Wine Cellar Design

WINE CELLAR Design

Schiffer Publishing Ltd®

4880 Lower Valley Road, Atglen, Pennsylvania 19310

Tina Skinner

Designed by Mark David Bowyer
Type set in Caslon 224 Bk BT / Humanist521 BT

ISBN: 978-0-7643-2862-6

Printed in China

Published by Schiffer Publishing Ltd.
4880 Lower Valley Road
Atglen, PA 19310
Phone: (610) 593-1777; Fax: (610) 593-2002
E-mail: Info@schifferbooks.com

For the largest selection of fine reference books on this and related subjects, please visit our web site at
www.schifferbooks.com
We are always looking for people to write books on new and related subjects. If you have an idea for a book please contact us at the above address.

This book may be purchased from the publisher.
Include $3.95 for shipping.
Please try your bookstore first.
You may write for a free catalog.

In Europe, Schiffer books are distributed by
Bushwood Books
6 Marksbury Ave.
Kew Gardens
Surrey TW9 4JF England
Phone: 44 (0) 20 8392-8585; Fax: 44 (0) 20 8392-9876
E-mail: info@bushwoodbooks.co.uk
Website: www.bushwoodbooks.co.uk
Free postage in the U.K., Europe; air mail at cost.

Contents

Drink No Wine Before Its Time   8

Building and Designing a Cellar   23

Build It Right the First Time   23

Options in Controlling Climate   46

Furnishing Your Cellar   64

Filling Your New Cellar   74

Resource Guide   220

Drink No Wine Before Its Time

By Art Stratemeyer

Wine is a living thing. It starts out young and brash, matures into something special and complex, and then eventually dies. This cycle can happen in a year, or in many decades. It all depends on two things – the wine itself – and the conditions it is stored in.

The majority of the wines sold today will taste better with a bit of aging. One way to demonstrate this is to purchase two bottles of an inexpensive red wine (perhaps a cabernet sauvignon). The morning of the day that you plan on having the wine, open one bottle and pour it into a decanter (a pitcher will do). Then, at dinner, open the second bottle and pour the two side by side. You will most likely note that the one you opened in the morning is a bit "softer" and has much more bouquet and complexity to the taste. This is often called "letting a wine breath," but it is also a simulation of how a wine will taste with aging.

The enemies of wine are heat, light, and vibration. Wine likes to be stored in a constant, cool temperature (around 58 degrees), in a dark place, and away from vibrations.

In today's world, the concept of a deep, dark, stone lined, wine "cellar" is often not a practical solution. With the advent of space-efficient cooling systems, you can now properly store wine in just about any location. Whether it is in an unfinished basement, bonus room, closet, garage, the corner of a den, or even within a credenza, the storage options are limited only by your imagination.

The driving factor on where and how you store your wine is mostly driven by the quantity that you want to be able to cellar. Today you can find self-contained units at many building centers that will store 25-100 bottles and fit under a kitchen counter or into a built-in. You can also find furniture-grade, self-contained units that can store upwards of 700-1000 bottles. With a custom made installation you can configure the cellar area in any manner that you wish.

A word of warning: whatever method you choose to store your wine, go bigger than you think you will need. Collecting wine can be a bit addictive and it's not hard to quickly outgrow a storage space.

Courtesy of Grotto Custom Wine Cellars & Cabinets

A glass wall provides visual access to a collection, set
apart in its own carefully controlled environment.
Courtesy of Wine Cellar Innovations

W**ine is the most healthful and most hygienic of beverages.**

~Louis Pasteur

Hanging wine glasses look decorative and make storage easy. This small cellar is tucked under a stairway. *Courtesy of WineRacks.com Inc.*

A wonderful, carved table and comfy chairs make this a welcoming center, perfect for sharing an uncorking with a dear friend. *Courtesy of Wine Cellar Innovations*

Imported limestone racking furnishes a showroom.
Courtesy of Dalst Stone Wine Cellars

A working counter caps case storage units.
Courtesy of Apex Wine Cellars & Racking Systems.

15

W ine improves with age. The older I get, the better I like it.

~Anonymous

An arched mural and a door with grape vines adds color and design. *Courtesy of WineRacks.com Inc.*

Glass doors and shelving share space with rich wood racking in a wine cellar that maximizes its potential for display.
Courtesy of Sleeping Grape Wine Cellars

A variety of storage racks follow the sage green walls of a distinguished cellar.
Courtesy of Doc Watters Wine Cellars, Inc.

A vaulted brick ceiling overlooks a cellar spacious enough to comfortably seat four for a little wine tasting. *Courtesy of Apex Wine Cellars & Racking Systems*

T emperature changes directly affect the chemical changes taking place in stored wine. The average temperature should be between 50 to 55 degrees Fahrenheit. Temperature should vary no more than 3 degrees a day and 5 degrees a year for the best results. Wines can age prematurely if there is too much change in temperature.

Rich tones and a shaded chandelier add to the stately sense of establishment in this cellar. The addition of a wet bar makes clean-up after uncorking and tasting a far simpler task. *Courtesy of Wine Cellar Innovations*

Temperature affects white wines more than red. Also, let wine sleep. Minimal movement is best, and vibrations should be limited.

Build It Right the First Time

By Doug M. Smith

I can't tell you how many times I've talked with wine collectors over the years that cut corners during the construction phase, and had problems with the function of their cellar soon after they put their first bottles into the racks. They all wished they had built it right the first time.

The common theme is either they never spent the time to research how to prepare the cellar, or they simply refused to listen to the advice of a qualified wine cellar consultant to save money. In most cases to fix the problem requires removal of all your wine, removal of the racking attached to the walls, and removal of the drywall or wood paneling to get inside the improperly prepared wall and ceiling cavity.

Another very common mistake is installing the wrong or undersized cooling equipment. This can be a very expensive fix, as you end up owning two cooling units. In both cases, the result is spending far more money to do it twice then doing it correctly from the outset.

Even though wine cellars are getting more and more popular they are still not everyday products that are installed into homes. Architects and builders just do not have enough experience to fully understand the fine construction details needed to make sure your valuable wine collection is properly stored. It is always recommended that you hire a qualified wine cellar consultant, such as one from Apex Wine Cellars, to make sure you are doing it right. To give you some basic assistance, below are some useful tips to make sure the cellar is built right.

Basic Design

The general rule for a cellar is that the thicker the walls, the better the insulation factor, the better the cellar remains at a consistent temperature. A vapor barrier is REQUIRED if a climate control cooling unit is installed to keep the cellar at the correct temperature. Six-millimeter plastic sheeting is applied to the HOT side of the cellar walls. All walls, ceiling and floor must be wrapped in plastic for a complete vapor barrier.

Building and Designing a Cellar

Graphics and Text
Courtesy of Vinotheque

The following steps and considerations for planning and building a wine cellar were developed by Vinotheque for use with their WhisperKool environmental control unit. The same basic considerations hold true for the design of any cellar in order to controlling temperature and humidity.

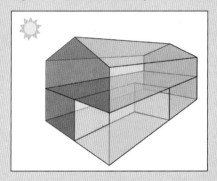

When positioning the cellar in your house, choose a room with access to adequate ventilation, and with limited exposure to direct sunlight. Determine which walls are inside and which will be outside. The WhisperKool system is designed to be mounted on an interior wall, and to vent into another room in the house. It can be mounted through an exterior wall and vent directly outside provided the climate is mild and exposure to sunlight and rain is limited.

Frame the room using standard 2x4 or 2x6 construction methods and ceiling joists that following standard local building practices. The thicker the wall and the thicker the insulation the better for maintaining a consistent temperature.

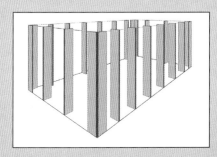

Apply 6 millimeter plastic sheeting to the warm side of the cellar walls to create a vapor barrier. Ideally, it should be applied to the exterior walls and ceiling. If it is impossible to get to the outside walls, then the plastic must be applied from inside the cellar. In high humidity areas, the barrier prevents warm, moist air from entering the cellar. Excessive moisture can cause mold to form. In dry areas, the barrier helps regulate humidity from within the cellar. It is impossible to overstate the importance of the vapor barrier.

Standard fiberglass or rigid foam insulation is most common, though blown-in insulation can also be used. A minimum of R-13 should be applied to the interior walls of the cellar. Exterior walls may require R-19. A minimum of R-19 is required for the ceiling, though if the ceiling is exposed to direct sunlight or strong winds, R-30 is required.

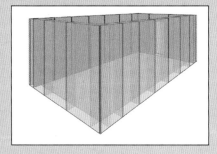

There are many options available for wall covering. Standard sheetrock is acceptable, but many cellar contractors prefer to use greenboard, which is moisture resistant and better suited to high humidity environments. A PVA paint formulation will provide a durable finish and help to work as a vapor barrier. Tongue-and-groove wood paneling is also an attractive option for wall covering. Rot resistant redwood and cedar are desirable as they breathe in the cool, damp environment of the cellar. Many finishing options are available for the wood. It is important to remember that spilled wine or water will discolor unfinished wood.

You may use many types of flooring including slate, tile, marble, and vinyl.

Insulation is REQUIRED on the walls and ceiling of a cellar. Standard "Fiberglass" or "Rigid Foam" insulation is commonly used in cellar construction. It is very important that all walls, ceiling and floor be insulated to keep the cellar temperature as consistent as possible during the summer and winter months.

In areas with high humidity, it is popular to apply foam insulation in all the walls, ceiling, and floor cavities to properly seal a cellar. This foam acts as both an insulation and vapor barrier. The important point to mention is there are several types of foam products on the market. A wine cellar must have "Closed Cell" foam. This type of foam will seal off the cellar from unwanted heat and moisture.

Interior walls and ceilings can be finished according to the decor theme of the cellar. Often drywall (green board) is applied, and then painted. Always use latex paint. It is also very common to apply wood paneling material to the walls and/or ceiling. This paneling is normally the same wood species as the racking material to create a uniform look throughout the cellar. Stone or granite can also be used as a wall covering material.

The cellar door needs to be an exterior grade, 1 3/4-inch, with weather stripping attached to all four sides of the door jamb. A bottom "sweep" or threshold is also needed. The door must have a very good seal to keep the cool cellar air from escaping. One of the most common problems with cooling units running continually is that doors have not been sealed properly. Glass doors and windows must have at least double pane-tempered glass. If the exterior room around the cellar is not an air-conditioned space, triple-pane glass is recommended.

Climate Controlled Systems

All the room preparations described above are very important. You can follow these instructions to the last detail, but if you do not choose the proper cooling equipment your cellar will not maintain the proper temperature and humidity levels. Thus, your valuable wine collection could be permanently harmed.

A cellar must keep a temperature of about 55 degrees Fahrenheit and humidity of 50-75 percent. There are several types of cooling equipment. Some of the criteria we use to determine which cooling equipment to use is

Carpet should not be used as it will mold and mildew in the cool, damp conditions of the cellar.

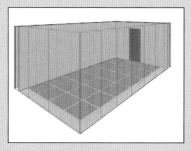

size and layout of your cellar, the number of bottles to be stored, geographic region, direction of the sun hitting exterior walls, glass doors or window, etc. It is advised that you consult a cellar design expert to specify the correct cooling system because there is no simple way to size units yourself. A consultant will conduct a "heat load" test on your cellar to help properly determine the proper size and configuration of cooling equipment required for your cellar. You don't want to cut corners with cooling equipment.

Some customers are shocked by the price of properly designed wine cellar cooling equipment. However, it is important to consider the value of your wine collection and not undersize or get talked into the wrong equipment that might save you a few bucks up front. Even a small, 500-bottle cellar can be valued at $20,000 plus. If you are unsure about the expertise of the company providing the equipment ask for references. What you are looking for is a qualified "refrigeration" contractor, not an HVAC contactor.

Cellar Monitoring Services

Make sure your prized wine collection is protected, around the clock and around the calendar. Wine collectors often have very busy lives. They are frequent travelers, have multiple collections in multiple locations, and simply can't take the time to inspect their cellar climate conditions on a regular basis.

It is recommended that you buy equipment that can monitor your cellar via the internet. These systems are similar to home fire and theft alarm systems. Some equipment like the CellarTec brand has monitoring built-in as standard equipment. All that is needed is a broadband connection or wireless connection in your home.

If your cellar cooling equipment does not have monitoring equipment or you have a passive cellar, there are stand-alone devices on the market that will monitor your cellar for you. One is called "CellarPod." Place the pod in your cellar and you are given a pass code protected website to view your air and liquid temperatures, humidity percentage, and light level (bright light is harmful to wine) of your cellar any time you have access to the internet. The CellarPod service will also notify you via email if conditions change in your cellar so you can take action to fix the problem before harm is done to your wine.

Install an exterior grade door using weather stripping on all four sides of the doorjamb. A bottom sweep or threshold is also required to create a tight seal and prevent cool air from escaping under the cellar door.

Many temperature and humidity control units were designed to fit between standard wall studs allowing installation with a minimum of modifications to existing wall structures. The unit should be placed close to the center of the room, on the chosen wall for ventilation. In the chosen location, cut a rectangular hole large enough to accommodate the unit, 12 inches below the ceiling.

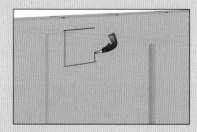

Sheetrock alone cannot support the weight of a 65 to a 110 lb. cooling unit, therefore it's important to frame the hole with 2x4s. Make sure the interior height remains the same as before. Once you have the frame built, you can install the unit following the instructions in the owner's manual.

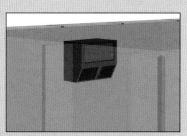

As with any sensitive electrical equipment, your climate control unit can be damaged by power surges and spikes, so you should use a surge protector or power conditioner. In addition, make sure that it has the proper starting amps to run at all times. Having other electrical components on the same circuit may compromise the units' ability to draw the necessary amperage needed to start. A backup generator is an important consideration in areas where there are frequent power outages due to storms or other circumstances.

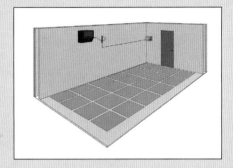

Lighting is an important aspect of cellar décor, however lights can produce a tremendous amount of heat, so some consideration must be made regarding their selection. Low voltage lights should be used to minimize the amount of heat generated. Canned ceiling lighting is popular in cellars, but attention to detail must be made to insure that the vapor barrier on the ceiling does not allow a loss of cool air and humidity. Track lighting can also be used to highlight display areas or artwork within the cellar. Timers and motion detector switches are recommended to prevent the lights being left on when no one is in the cellar.

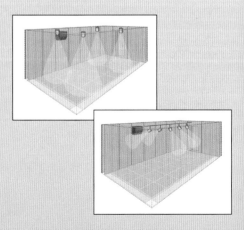

Duel displays of half-round shelves form a focal point in this cellar.
Courtesy of Wine Cellar Innovations

Proper ventilation on the exhaust side of the cooling unit is one of the most important considerations in building your cellar. The WhisperKool System is designed to cool up to 30 degrees colder than the temperature on the exhaust side of the unit. Therefore, in order to maintain 55 degrees in the cellar, the exhaust room must not get warmer than 85 degrees. In the cellar, cool air comes down out of the unit at a 45 degree angle, causing the warmer air to rise toward the ceiling. This is then pulled into the unit providing a consistent temperature throughout. As the unit cools the cellar it generates at least as much heat on the exhaust side. Thus adequate airflow must be available to allow the heat to dissipate.

Although it is not recommended, the climate control unit can be mounted through an exterior wall under the following circumstances. 1. As long as the temperature does not exceed 85 degrees in the summer or go below 40 degrees in the winter. Typically, no one would operate a cooling unit in the winter for obvious reasons. But central heating inside the home can cause cellar temperatures to rise in winter months.

Even in a temperate climate, the rear of the unit must be protected from rain and direct sunlight. Protective housing should be provided for the unit on the exterior of the home to prevents moisture and direct heat from penetrating it.

If the warm air in the exhaust room is not ventilated, the exhaust room will gradually become warmer. Since the cooling unit can only maintain a 30 degree temperature difference, this will

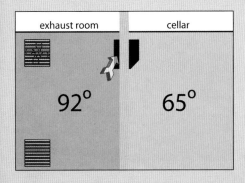

27

cause the temperature in the cellar to rise as well. Inadequate ventilation is the most common mistake consumers make when installing the unit. This causes the cooling unit to run continuously, and may lead to additional problems such as icing over or premature failure. To prevent this, an exhaust fan must be installed in the room to remove the warm trapped air. However, there must be a fresh air intake source installed as well, otherwise air lock, or lack of air flow. will prevent the room from cooling. Do not attempt to install ducting on the unit. The fans are not designed to push air through a restricted environment. Adequate ventilation and airflow will assure consistent temperatures in the cellar, maximize the cooling unit's performance, and improve longevity.

For proper wine storage, the goal is to maintain relative humidity between 50 and 70 percent. In high humidity environments, the unit will remove excess humidity out of the air and dissipate this moisture through the condensate evaporator system or optional drain line. However, if you live in a dry environment, you may need to create humidity within the cellar. This can be done by the periodic use of a non-heat humidifier or by installing a small decorative fountain within the cellar.

Wine racking can vary significantly based on your style, taste, budget and use of the cellar. Racking is usually made from mahogany, redwood, or cedar. Attention should be focused on bottle sizes, storage capacity, and display options. Some cellars are designed simply for one purpose, to store wine. Others are built to showcase a nice collection and entertain friends. Wine accessory catalogs offer a variety of economical and easy to use racking kits to meet your needs. Or, cellar contractors offer design, manufacturing, and installation services, which range from the purely functional to the highly elaborate.

Once the racking is installed, you will have created a beautiful home and safe environment for your collection.

In the style of an old Spanish keep, a stone alcove sits at the base of cellar stairs, its tile roof overlooked by a balcony. The stone is actually a manufactured product, with wood racking and a wrought iron door rounding out the impressive presentation. *Courtesy of Eldorado Stone.*

A newly racked wine cellar sits, awaiting a proud owner's first picks to fill its beckoning shelves. *Courtesy of Borrowing Owl Winery*

W hat is better than to sit at the end of the day and drink wine with friends!

~James Joyce

A work counter separates shelves and creates a place for display wine. *Courtesy of Sleeping Grape Wine Cellars*

Shaped like a grape cluster, a unique light casts its glow on this spacious cellar. *Courtesy of Wine Cellar Innovations*

A large wall mural of a vineyard is framed by a symmetrical rise of racks on either side. Two built-in wall racks above a tile mural allow for the display of special treasures. *Courtesy of Wine Cellar Innovations*

Courtesy of Eldorado Stone

A wet bar was fashioned from the cross-section of a tree set atop wine barrels, which open to serve as handy storage. *Courtesy of Apex Wine Cellars & Racking Systems*

W ine is bottled poetry.

~Robert Louise Stevenson

Take a trip back in time with a display that duplicate wine vaults of centuries ago. A bar accommodates half a dozen tasters beneath an impressive stone ceiling. *Courtesy of Dalst Stone Wine Cellars*

Courtesy of Sleeping Grape Wine Cellars

A stone floor and brick walls set a solid stage for a wonderful collection of racking by Atwood Fine Architectural Cabinetry. An antechamber offers a place to rest and sample the collection. *Courtesy of Steven Paul Whitsitt Photography*

I t is helpful to buy wine in sequence. Buy some that will be drunk quickly and some that you plan on aging. Most wine is meant to be consumed quickly.

The passageways to a wine storage area are appropriately medieval, setting the tone for the treasures stored beyond. Hand-hewn beams support the ceiling, and the cellar is lit by sconces crafted from hand-forged iron.
Courtesy of Germano Custom Wine Cellars

y purchasing case lots, you will be able to follow the progress of a wine as it ages, and discover when it is at its best.

This carefully crafted wine cellar allows the owner to display the wine above the racks where they are stored. It makes searching for the right bottle of wine easier. *Courtesy of Grotto Custom Wine Cellars & Cabinets*

Racking has been carefully fitted within a natural stone surround in a cellar.
Courtesy of Vicarage Wine Cellars

Purchasing cases of wine not only saves you money, it is also a great investment opportunity. *Courtesy of Apex Wine Cellars & Racking Systems*

Courtesy of Grotto Custom Wine Cellars & Cabinets

Options in Controlling Climate

By Art Stratemeyer

Wine likes to be stored at a constant, cool temperature. The "ideal" temperature is 55-60 degrees. If you want multi-decade storage, or you are storing wines for resale, then try 55 degrees. However, if you want the wine to age and peak within a timeline where you will actually be drinking it, a 58-60 degree range is best.

One thing to remember is that your home cooling and/or a window air conditioner will not provide the "constant" temperature that is required. Remember, the more attention you pay to insulation, sealing, and vapor barriers the less work the cooling unit will have to do. Assuming you don't open the door to the cellar, a cooling unit should only have to run 2-3 times a day.

There are many ways of cooling a cellar. The following are the most common. Whichever system you choose, like anything else you buy, take the time to do a bit of research about the supplier.

Self-contained units: These units look like small air conditioners. They have been used in thousands of cellars and there are several manufacturers. They all mount through the wall of the cellar area. On the pro side, these units are easy to install, cost efficient, and produce relatively little noise (think of 4-6 computer fans running).

On the con side, they are sealed units that can only be repaired at the factory. Also, they have an upper limit to the cubic footage they will cool, they must exhaust into an adjacent room and thus add noise to that space, and they protrude within the cellar space and are hard to hide.

Split systems: These are systems where the compressor is located away from the cellar and only the evaporator/cooling fans are within the cellar. On the positive side, they produce less noise and, since the cooling unit is within the cellar there is no noise in adjacent rooms. They also have greater capacity, with many being sized to handle larger cellars. These kinds of systems, installed by local refrigeration companies, can be serviced locally.

On the con side, freon and condensate lines must be run from the cellar unit to the external compressor; the cooling unit is usually ceiling mounted within the cellar and is hard to hide, and they cost more than self contained units

Ducted systems: These systems are self-contained units that duct the cool air into the wine cellar. On the positive side, they produce the least noise because there are no fans and/or units within the cellar; they are totally self-contained; they can handle larger cellars, and local refrigeration companies can repair most units. Aesthetically, only a supply and a return grill is visible in the cellar.

Drawbacks to ducted systems include a higher purchase price and the need to run ductwork to the cellar. This is probably not cost efficient for small cellars.

Moisture control and humidity: You will most likely have read that there is a "preferred" humidity for storing your wine. This number was arrived at simply by someone noting the humidity of the limestone caves in France where wine is stored. If you ask three wine lovers about what the right humidity should be, you would most likely get three different answers. Mine is quite simple. Unless you are building a cellar in the Sahara Desert you really don't need to worry about adding any humidity. I've maintained cellars around the United States for over thirty years and have never found it to be an issue.

Where you do have a humidity issue is in those cases where you have too much humidity. Then you start getting issues of moisture build-up, moldy labels, and mildewed walls. Also, if you have added a humidification unit, it needs to be continually monitored to insure that the humidity is not getting too high.

Today's cooling units are designed to maintain a constant humidity without removing too much moisture. A standard air conditioner cools by removing moisture and drying the air. Thus the cooling units for wine cellars are designed to make sure the humidity does not get too high, while not taking excessive moisture out of the air.

Whichever unit you choose to use, you will need to provide some drainage for excess moisture from the unit. Even the self-contained ones that say they "burn off" excess moisture still provide for external drainage just in case the moisture gets too high.

47

C ome, come, good wine is a good familiar creature if it be well used; exclaim no more against it.

~William Shakespeare

Steel grape vines adorn the glass portal to this lovely wine cellar.
Courtesy of Apex Wine Cellars & Racking Systems

A wine cellar accomodates a mixed display, and provides storage for oversize bottles. *Courtesy of Artistic Wine Cellars*

Courtesy of WineRacks.com Inc.

Courtesy of Rosehill Wine Cellars

Courtesy of Doc Watters Wine Cellars, Inc.

Courtesy of Valentini's Custom Wine Cellars

A glorious expanse of wine cellar plays host to a huge collection, and serves as an impressive retreat. *Courtesy of Artistic Wine Cellar*

I love everything that's old: old friends, old times, old manners, old books, old wine.

~Oliver Goldsmith

This wine cellar puts a variety of display styles to task, adding visual interest. *Courtesy of Grotto Custom Wine Cellars & Cabinets*

Granite counters provide workspace within an open wine storage room, and underline a view into the family room beyond.
Courtesy of Apex Wine Cellars & Racking Systems

oncrete heats up and cools down slowly, making basements an ideal location for wine storage.

Courtesy of Doc Watters Wine Cellars, Inc.

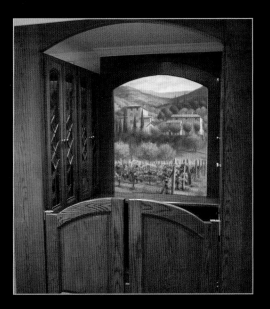

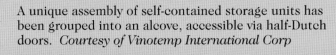

A unique assembly of self-contained storage units has been grouped into an alcove, accessible via half-Dutch doors. *Courtesy of Vinotemp International Corp*

A newly constructed wine storage unit provides an impressive foray beyond the concrete walls of a cellar. *Courtesy of Sleeping Grape Wine Cellars*

The aroma of grapes diminishes as wine ages and is replaced by the smell of ripe fruit, cedar, chocolate, etc. Also, the tannins in the wine cluster together to make the wine easier to drink.

Wrought iron walls off a wine cellar designed by Rick Ginder of Designerick.com. *Courtesy of Wellborn Forest Fine Kitchen Cabinetry*

Courtesy of Grotto Custom Wine Cellars & Cabinets

A collection includes specialty bottles, accounted for in racking installed to accommodate the owner's taste for the unusual. *Courtesy of Apex Wine Cellars & Racking Systems*

A curved configuration adds interest to a newly-installed stretch of racking.
Courtesy of Apex Wine Cellars & Racking Systems

B ordeaux, burgundy, and vintage champagnes can double or triple in value after several years.

Courtesy of Grotto Custom Wine Cellars & Cabinets

Furnishing Your Cellar

By Art Stratemeyer

O nce you have created the space for your wines, the enjoyment of designing the racking, bins, display units, etc. for the space follows. The rising popularity of wine cellars over the past decade has given rise to an entire industry that supplies the needed racking. A simple search for "wine racking" on the internet will result in hundreds of choices. Basically you have the following choices in racking:

Kits: there are many suppliers that will ship you the racking in kit form and if you are a bit handy with tools you can then assemble the racking yourself.

Factory installed: Here the supplier will work with you on the design using their standard racking and then, depending on the supplier, they use their own installers or hire local contractors.

Custom made: This is where a craftsman, like myself, works with you on the design and then custom-makes and installs all of the racking.

Racking Terminology

Single deep racking: Each "cell" of the racking holds one bottle
Double deep racking: Each "cell" holds two bottles, one in front of the other
Strength: Insure that the racking is made with sound manufacturing techniques. Remember, a thousand-bottle cellar can hold close to 4,000 pounds of wine. The racking should be soundly constructed and should provide for strong attachment to the walls of your cellar.
Size: If possible, you should select racking that is a full 13 inches deep (26 inches for double deep) so that the entire bottle is encased in the racking. There are racks that are only 9 inches deep, but they leave the necks of the bottles exposed and these can easily be knocked against when walking close to the racking. Another very important factor is what "standard" bottle size the racking will hold. In an effort to have the most "bottles per foot" of racking, several suppliers offer their racking for "standard" bottles. This generally means the "Bordeaux" shaped (square shouldered) bottles. I've been in many cellars where the user has found that the "Burgundy" shaped (squat, slope-shouldered) will not fit into the "standard" openings. This means that your favorite Pinots, Rhones, some Italians, etc. will not fit.

Height: The maximum height of the racking should be around 90-92 inches. Anything over that will require some kind of a step stool or ladder to reach the upper bottles.

Materials: Here you have an almost unlimited choice of woods. There is a false notion that you need a "moisture resistant" wood. In the majority of cases the humidity of the room will be approximately the ambient humidity of your home (see the Cooling and Humidity section) so moisture resistance is not needed. About the only wood(s) you want to avoid are those that are highly scented, like aromatic cedar. You don't want the scent getting into the wine. If the racking is going to be in a basement and/or directly on concrete then you should use treated wood as a "base" to elevate the racking.

Special sized bottle formats: Depending on the wines you collect, you will also need some racking sized for "non-standard" bottles. As a minimum, I recommend some amount of racking for sparkling wines and possibly magnums. Also, it is nice to plan ahead and have some racking for half-bottle sizes (dessert wines, splits, etc.)

Display racking: Often people want to be able to display special bottles of wine. With some factory made and all custom solutions you can create just about any style that you want.

Diamonds and bin storage: These can provide a nice aesthetic touch to a wine cellar and can also provide efficient case storage. However, you need to be aware that, while they look very "space efficient," in fact they are very poor in this area. As an example: if the openings in a diamond will hold sixteen bottles, you need to keep in mind that, eventually you will mix wines in these openings and getting out one of the lower ones means taking all of the others out first. Also, there is a safety factor you need to know about! If you store any "slope shouldered" (i.e. Pinot Noir, Champagne, etc.) bottles in these, it is not a matter of "if," but rather a matter of "when" a bottle will fall out and crash to the floor. The only bottles that rest safely in these styles of storage are the "square shouldered" (Bordeaux style) bottles. Even then you have to be careful when removing bottles.

Courtesy of Apex Wine Cellars & Racking Systems

Restaurant patrons gain visual access to the establishment's collection through glass walls.
Courtesy of Wine Cellar Innovations

A carved, double door guards a carefully crafted wine keep beyond.
Within, a stone wall and slate flooring play host to a collection of wood
racking. *Courtesy of Sleeping Grape Wine Cellars*

W ine is made to be drunk as women are made to be loved; profit by the freshness of youth or the splendor of maturity; do not await decrepitude."

~*Theophile Malvezin*

S et aside wines bottled the year your children were born. It makes a lovely coming of age gift. Likewise, wedding anniversaries are well celebrated with wines conceived in the same year.

Golden tones infuse this new cellar. *Courtesy of Sleeping Grape Wine Cellars*

W

ine that maketh glad the heart of man.

~*The Book of Psalms, 104:15*

Wine has traditionally aged in stone cellars in oak barrels.
Courtesy of Vicarage Wine Cellars

Wine Cellars & Racking Systems

Filling Your New Cellar

By Art Stratemeyer

Once you have completed your cellar space. Now comes the fun part: filling it! The best advice I can offer is "Take your time."

There is the desire to go right out and start buying wines to put into the new cellar. Some 35 years ago when I started collecting I did just the same thing. Now, decades later I chuckle at some of the wines in my cellar (some of which died long ago) and say to myself, "why the heck did I buy that wine?" My early wine buying strategy was like mapping out a set of varicose veins: no rhyme or reason.

Unless you are purchasing wines for investment, you should focus on buying the wines that you like, not those recommended by some magazine. Remember, no two individuals' palates are the same. You are buying wines to drink for your own enjoyment and not because of an arbitrary "score" from a magazine.

Take the time to educate yourself. Many wines are made to be drunk within 1-5 years, while others might not reach their true potential for 10-20 years. Unless you truly know the wine, don't start buying by the caseload right away. Each vintage brings new and different aspects to a wine no matter the producer.

Have fun experimenting with wines in your cellar. Let some age a bit and see what happens. Many times I have pulled a bottle of inexpensive wine from my cellar that I had totally forgotten about and assumed it was dead, only to find it was amazing and still quite alive! Let some whites age a bit. If you've never had an aged white Burgundy (chardonnay) you will be amazed at the delicious complexity that white wines can develop.

Track Your Wines

You've taken the time to invest in a cellar, so you should develop a method for keeping track of your wines and tasting notes that go with them. In today's world, with the idea of keeping a "diary" almost gone, I can't tell you what a pleasure it is to be able to look back on decades worth of notes about wines I've drunk. I also included in my notes the food I had with them and the people with whom I shared them.

On the practical side, you want to be able to actually find the wines in your cellar. You also want to keep track of when they will possibly be going bad to help prevent the proverbial "dead soldier" wines that we all find in a cellar from time to time. You can do this simply with a cellar notebook where you record the locations and tasting notes of the wines in your cellar. With computers, you can use a spreadsheet or homemade database or you can purchase one of the commercially available software programs designed for tracking your wine.

Placing your wine in the cellar

All too often I see new collectors (and I did this myself early on) say "Ok, I'll put my California Cabs in this section, my California whites in another section, my Bordeaux in another section, etc." This might work in the beginning, but it will soon become cumbersome. Imagine your wine cellar like a set of bookshelves. If you keep only science fiction on one shelf and history on the shelf below it, what do you do when the science fiction shelf fills up and you want to add more books there? You need to move all of the history books first or create another shelf in perhaps another bookcase. The best way I've found over the years (assuming you have the discipline to record where you put your wines) is simply to place bottles in any open "slots" with no regard to the type of wine. My chaos theory is the best way.

Purchasing / Drinking Strategy

This varies depending on the individual. Over the years, I've seldom bought a full case of any given wine. Instead I've used three strategies for buying and drinking wines that I want to cellar:

Wines that I know well and want to have: I buy one bottle for tasting, then if I like it, I usually buy four to six bottles. Drink one later in the year of purchasing. The next about two years later and from my notes on that wine I set the years for drinking the rest of them. I usually reserve one to two bottles for the longest aging just to see how they do. This is a bit risky as I might guess wrong but it is a great treat when you guess right.

Wines that are new to me: I first buy one bottle, open it and let it breath for most of a day and then taste it. If I decide I want some for cellaring I will buy three bottles and stage them out over the years for drinking.

Every day wines: You need to have a separate section for everyday wines that you might not want to take the time to record into your book. This should be an area where you or your spouse can grab a wine without worrying if it is meant for collecting.

Years ago, I learned this the hard way. I had returned home from a trip and my lovely wife mentioned that she had her bridge group over and that they really loved the "chardonnays" that were served and wondered where they could buy them. I looked on the counter and there sat six empty 1976 Montrachet bottles! This is a fairly rare white Burgundy, and was valued at that point at around $500 per bottle. Seeing the look on my face, my wife immediately said "I hope I didn't open any good ones." Being a good husband, I simply said, "Well, yes you drank some fairly good ones," but it was not until years later that I told her their true value. The next day I immediately created a "you can pull any wine from here" section in my cellar.

Courtesy of Apex Wine Cellars & Racking Systems

75

A wine cellar welcomes those who journey to the base of the stairs, its own unique destination on a lower floor of the home. *Courtesy of Wine Cellar Innovations*

More than 20 million acres are cultivated around the world for wine grape production, making it the number one fruit crop. The most populous varietal is Airén, claiming over one million acres in central Spain. It makes a mediocre white wine, and a very nice brandy.

A glass-topped display case makes visual identification of a collection easier.
Courtesy of Apex Wine Cellars & Racking Systems

Courtesy of Grotto Custom Wine Cellars & Cabinets

A vibrant ceiling mural adds color to a room packed with racking. A central worktable, capped with glass, provides visual access to the treasures aging just below. *Courtesy of Apex Wine Cellars & Racking Systems*

A granite counter culminates the ingress of a compact cellar, crowned by a convex ceiling. *Courtesy of Rosehill Wine Cellars*

A handsome entrance sets the tone for the collection beyond. *Courtesy of Apex Wine Cellars & Racking Systems*

A narrow central work table permits plenty of aisle way access between three
walls packed with racking. *Courtesy of Wine Cellar Innovations*

JUSTIN
Vineyards & Winery

2001

PASO ROBLES

77% CABERNET SAUVIGNON
13% CABERNET FRANC
10% MERLOT
(unfiltered)

ISOSCELES

GROWN · PRODUCED ·
AND · BOTTLED · BY
JUSTIN VINEYARDS & WINERY
11680 CHIMNEY ROCK ROAD
PASO ROBLES, CA 93446 USA
Alc. 14.5% by Volume

Beige tones unify a cellar designed for serious storage. Racked floor to ceiling, the owners incrporated a seciton designated for case storage, and allotted only a little space to showy display. *Courtesy of Artistic Wine Cellars*

C ork was developed as a seal for bottles in the late 17th Century. Only after this were bottles set on their side for aging. Bottle shapes slowly evolved from short and bulbous to tall and slender.

An rack set at an angle, terminates in a round countertop. This configuration forms a centerpiece for a compact room converted to a wine cellar.
Courtesy of Apex Wine Cellars & Racking Systems

T oasting became popular in the 6th Century B.C. in Greece. By drinking first from a common decanter to prove the wine was not poisoned, a host could then offer drinks all around and assure that it was with good intents for everyone's health. By the 1800s, toasting was so popular that it was considered rude to refrain from a toast. Moreover, everyone at the table would have a drink dedicated to them, as omission of a guest was considered contemptuous.

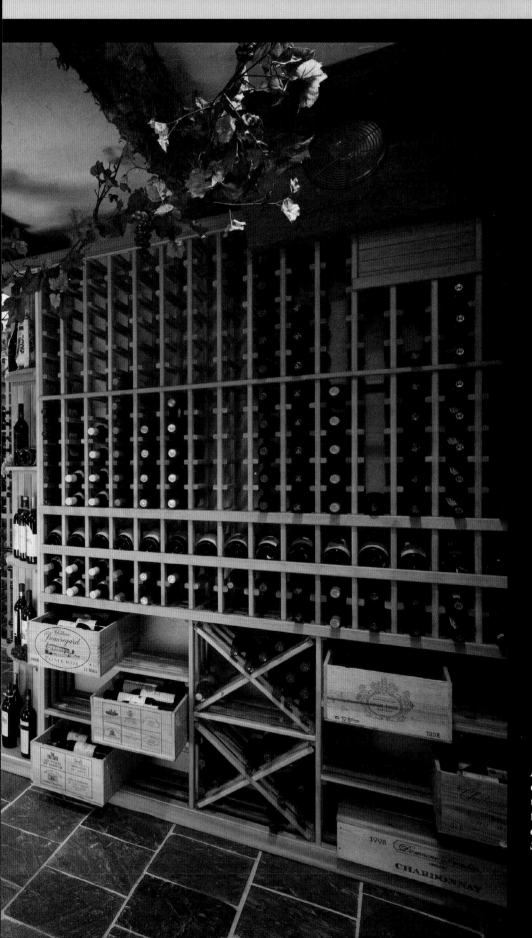

A copper vessel sink and beamed ceiling add country charm to this efficient cellar, composed of floor-to-ceiling racking. *Courtesy of Apex Wine Cellars & Racking Systems*

Courtesy of WineRacks.com Inc.

A narrow central work table permits plenty of aisle way access between three walls packed with racking. *Courtesy of Wine Cellar Innovations*

A large wall mural of a vineyard is framed by a symmetrical rise of racks on either side. Two built-in wall racks above a tile mural allow for the display of special treasures. *Courtesy of Wine Cellar Innovations*

Purchasing cases of wine not only saves you money, but is also a great opportunity for investment. *Courtesy of Apex Wine Cellars & Racking Systems*

94

Two rooms, one with a tasting area, have been set aside to carefully store selected vintages amidst limestone shelving. *Courtesy of Dalst Stone Wine Cellars*

Curves round out the corners and add visual interest to this room. *Courtesy of Wine Cellar Innovations*

A gorgeous painting, copper sink, and an attractive hanging lamp add welcoming touches to this wine cellar.
Courtesy of Rosehill Wine Cellars

Constructed in a walk-out basement, a window treatment will be the last piece of furnishing provided for this handsome new cellar prior to stocking it. Courtesy of Sleeping Grape Wine Cellars

W hen pouring sparkling wine, first pour an ounce into the cup and allow it to settle. Then pour the remainder of the serving into the initially poured wine and it will not foam as much.

Carefully covered wall sconces prevent harmful light from contaminating delicate, developing wines. *Courtesy of Apex Wine Cellars & Racking Systems*

A richly detailed door opens to a cellar that exceeds expectations. Within, different styles of racking provide visual interest, while packing maximum storage into the room. The cellar includes a sloped central storage unit that fills the center of the room, culminating in a work counter illuminated by a wonderful chandelier. *Courtesy of Apex Wine Cellars & Racking Systems*

W ine has so many organic chemical compounds it is considered more complex than blood serum.

Various views explore a wonderful wine vault, from the arched wooden doorway set within a stone surround, to the richly detailed interior. A mural acts as the focal point, evoking a Tuscan vineyard. Slotted racks as well as arched shelves crafted from used wine barrels help house an impressive collection. Details, liked carved drawer pulls, attest to the owner's sensibilities. Continued on next page... *Courtesy of Apex Wine Cellars & Racking Systems*

A mural acts as the focal point, evoking a Tuscan vineyard. Slotted racks as well as arched shelves crafted from used wine barrels help house an impressive collection. Details, liked carved drawer pulls, attest to the owner's sensibilities. *Courtesy of Apex Wine Cellars & Racking Systems*

W ine breathes, so be sure to provide a clean storage area. A well ventilated room, free of musty smells, is essential.

Just as one would expect to find in a newly-built castle, a long passageway leads through aisles of wine racking, culminating in a resting spot where one can enjoy a selection found along the journey. *Courtesy of Wine Cellar Innovations*

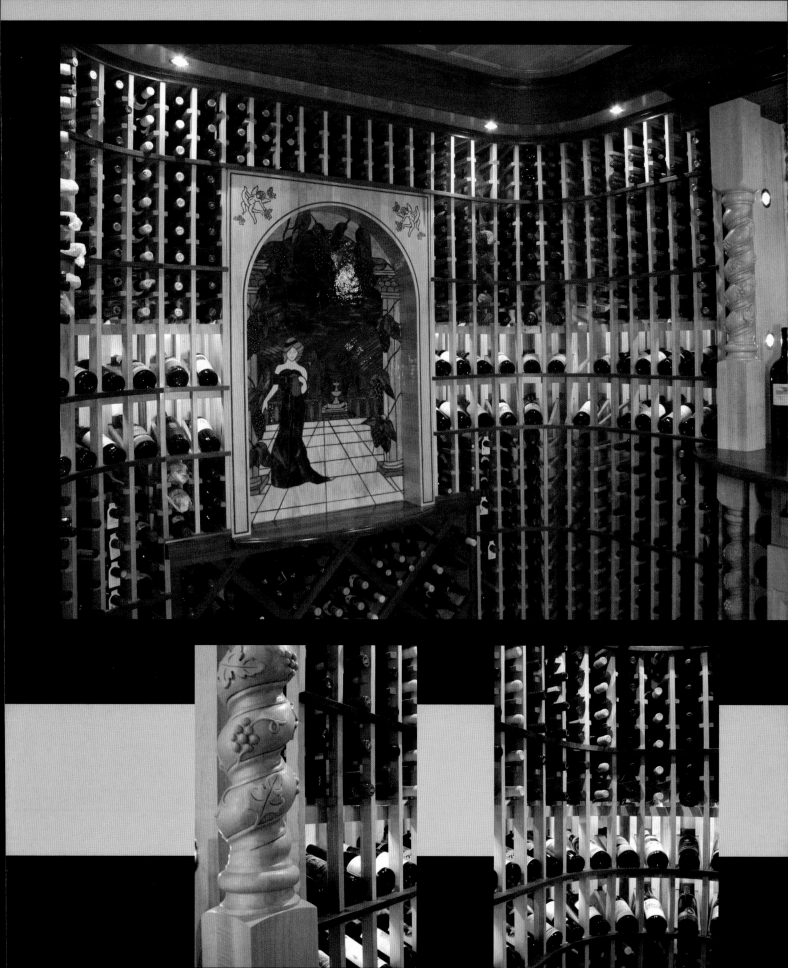

This wine cellar features a lot of fascinating artwork in addition to an impressive collection of wine. The selection of a blonde wood finish for the racking and carved details helps brighten the room and expand the sense of space. *Courtesy of Wine Cellar Innovations*

Horizontal storage is best. This keeps the wine in contact with the cork. It also avoids deposits of sediment on the bottom of the bottle.

A busy cellar owner has left lots of space for stacking full cases of wine, keeping the cellar tidy between work sessions to unpack and document the collection. *Courtesy of Wine Cellar Innovations*

Y ou are protecting your wine from all the elements, light being one of them. Mercury, sodium, or neon lamps are preferable to fluorescent lighting.

A marvelous stone floor perfectly complements the racking in this cellar. The central rack stair-steps to the ceiling, preserving the open feel of the room. A practical table culminates in a semi-circular end with quarter round shelves, creating a welcome gathering place for visiting friends and family. *Courtesy of Wine Cellar Innovations*

Two rooms allow the collector two environments to control in order to more perfectly age wines with differing requirements. *Courtesy of Wine Cellar Innovations*

A tiled floor has been customized to celebrate wine.
Courtesy of Wine Cellar Innovations

Courtesy of Apex Wine Cellars & Racking Systems

Double glass doors provide visual access to a wonderful circular cellar, still so new that most of its collection resides in cases on the lower shelves. A cathedral ceiling adds to the spacious effect. *Courtesy of Wine Cellar Innovations*

Your refrigerator is no place to store wine, even short term! The door opens frequently, and the temperature fluctuations are damaging. The smells are liable to affect your wine. And the temperature is most likely too cold for proper aging.

A back-lit stained-glass window brings gaiety to a gorgeous brick cellar. *Courtesy of Wine Cellar Innovations*

The art of vineyard cases, as well as a fanciful wine barrel table, compete with a tile mural amidst the many racks of wine in a cellar designed by C. R. White. Courtesy of *Steven Paul Whitsitt*

W ine is a living liquid containing no preservatives. Its life cycle comprises youth, maturity, old age, and death. When not treated with reasonable respect it will sicken and die.

~Julia Child

Curving shelves maximize the utility
of a small space. *Courtesy of Apex
Wine Cellars & Racking Systems*

An opened bottle of wine improperly stored overnight will oxidize and you will not be able to drink it. You can try to store it with vacuum corking, though it won't work for very long and some wines may turn flat or dull because of this. Gassing works best, though it is not foolproof. Transferring the wine to a smaller bottle helps minimize oxygen in the bottle.

Courtesy of Grotto Custom Wine Cellars & Cabinets

A stainless steel racking system and walls work together for a striking, futuristic effect in this modern storage unit. *Courtesy of Alan's Wine Cellar*

An arched window offers a view into a
cellar, half full of maturing wines.
Courtesy of Wine Cellar Innovations

lush, rose, and
dry white wines
should be main-
tained at temperatures
between 46-57 degrees
Fahrenheit; Champagne
and sparkling wines at 43-
47 degrees; light red wine
at about 55 degrees, and
deep read wines between
59-66 degrees.

Two stained-glass windows help decorate this wine cellar.
A stepladder provides quick access to the higher bottles.
Courtesy of Wine Cellar Innovations

Spotlights highlight the various racking options within this wonderful cellar.
Courtesy of Doc Watters Wine Cellars, Inc.

Right:
Spotlights highlight the various
racking options within this
wonderful cellar. Courtesy of Doc
Watters Wine Cellars, Inc.

ewly planted
vineyards take
four to five
years to produce a com-
mercial crop. Grapevine
varietals can not be repro-
duced reliably from seed,
but must be grafted.

Mixing and matching storage rack designs gives this wine cellar a more appealing look. *Courtesy of Valentini's Custom Wine Cellars*

S toring wine that will be consumed within six months is much like storing it long term. It needs to be carefully protected, on its side, at stable temperatures and humidity.

This carefully crafted wine cellar allows the owner to display the wine above the racks where they are stored. It makes searching for the right bottle of wine easier. *Courtesy of Grotto Custom Wine Cellars & Cabinets*

Tucked off the stair landing, a door emphasizes the fortification provided for precious vintages stored beyond. *Courtesy of Grotto Custom Wine Cellars & Cabinets*

137

It is hot atop the refrigerator. It also tends to be closer to the light, and the area is vibrated every time the refrigerator or freezer doors are opened. Don't store wine there.

Cabinetry was carefully crafted and stacked to accommodate this basement storage room's central occupant, a boulder. Stackable storage racks make it possible to fit shelves into any area. *Courtesy of Sleeping Grape Wine Cellars*

Glass doors and shelving share space with rich wood racking in a wine cellar that maximizes its potential for display. *Courtesy of Sleeping Grape Wine Cellars*

Corks preserve best in 70 percent humidity. If they become too dry, air will enter the bottle. Too much moisture will damage bottle labels. It may cause mold to grow, or the labels to separate from the bottles.

Courtesy of Doc Watters Wine Cellars, Inc.

A new cellar awaits future acquisitions. Colorful accessories accent the blonde racking.
Courtesy of Sleeping Grape Wine Cellars

Courtesy of WineRacks.com Inc.

A narrow island work center adds extra storage to a space dedicated to maximizing the bottle count. One concession has been made in the form of a decorative archway, adorned as an altar to the mighty grape. *Courtesy of Apex Wine Cellars & Racking Systems*

Courtesy of WineRacks.com Inc.

Simulated candles illuminate a mirrored archway.
Courtesy of Artistic Wine Cellars

A cedar ceiling aids in moisture and pest-control in a carefully crafted cellar. *Courtesy of Wine Cellar Innovations*

Temperatures below 55 degrees slow the aging of wine. Light-struck wine tends to taste and smell like wet cardboard. Avoid putting wines near fluorescent lights, especially delicate whites. Most modern wine bottles have built-in filters to protect the contents from UV rays, but long-term exposure to light will still penetrate.

A butterfly beautifies the view from within a cellar at Stone Mountain Vineyard in California. *Courtesy of Wine Cellar Innovations*

A central storage area for cases is capped with a stair-step rise for display bottles. *Courtesy of Wine Cellar Innovations*

The curved corner of this wine rack allows for easy entrance into the cellar. *Courtesy of Wine Cellar Innovations*

Wrought iron walls off a wine cellar designed by Rick Ginder of Designerick.com.
Courtesy of Wellborn Forest Fine Kitchen Cabinetry

Built for business, this cellar packs bottles floor to ceiling, including case storage on the floor. *Courtesy of Alan's Wine Cellar*

A crest-like wood carving adds an air of authenticity.
Courtesy of Alan's Wine Cellar

A wall-length display row provides visual access to special
bottles. Mirrors add light and a sense of space to cellar areas.
Courtesy of Alan's Wine Cellar

Wine crates were recycled to create paneling above wine racks.
Glass grapes adorn a beautiful stained glass lighting fixture.
Courtesy of Wine Cellar Innovations

*Courtesy of Grotto Custom Wine
Cellars & Cabinets*

A newly constructed wine storage unit provides an impressive foray beyond the concrete walls of a cellar. *Courtesy of Sleeping Grape Wine Cellars*

An island work station doubles as an entertainment area on special occasions when close friends are invited to sample the progress of selected vintage. *Courtesy of Wine Cellar Innovations*

Shaped like a grape cluster, a unique light casts its glow on this spacious cellar. *Courtesy of Wine Cellar Innovations*

Quarter-round end caps allow for a pretty display in shelves close to a leaded-glass door and sidelights. *Courtesy of Wine Cellar Innovations*

Courtesy of Sleeping Grape Wine Cellars

Bar stools and a small table provide a forum for wine-loving friends to gather and enjoy the collection. *Courtesy of Apex Wine Cellars & Racking Systems*

If you are uncorking several bottles for an evening's activities, make sure to serve your younger vintages first. Older wines are more flavorful and will overpower the youngsters. Likewise, serve light-bodied before full-bodied, white before red, dry before sweet.

A wall mural provides a window-like view to a vineyard, sans the sunlight that is unwanted here. *Courtesy of Wine Cellar Innovations*

Wrought iron and a redwood finish characterize this new cellar. *Courtesy of Sleeping Grape Wine Cellars*

Racking follows a rising ceiling angle, as a collection finds its way under
the cellar stairs. The area was designed by David Frym of Northbay Kitchen.
Courtesy of Steven Paul Whitsitt Photography

The table is set for a tasting amidst a beautifully stocked cellar.
Courtesy of Artistic Wine Cellars

160

An expansive granite coun-tertop includes a peninsula for added work-space. *Courtesy of Apex Wine Cellars & Rack-ing Systems*

A rich rosewood finish on the racking reflects the spotlights. *Courtesy of WineRacks.com Inc.*

Courtesy of Doc Watters Wine Cellars, Inc.

Hanging wine glasses look decorative and make storage
easy. This small cellar is tucked under a stairway.
Courtesy of WineRacks.com Inc.

163

A vaulted brick ceiling and stone floor evoke the authentic atmosphere of an old world wine cellar. *Courtesy of Burrowing Owl Winery*

S mall spaces set off larger rooms, wine alcoves provide their contents with careful protections, while keeping them near and dear, and often within eyesight. Here are wonderful examples of how a lot of storage was created by chipping away a little bit from a larger room.

A glass wall provides visual access to a collection, set apart in its own carefully controlled environment. *Courtesy of Wine Cellar Innovations*

A cellar takes up a minimum amount of floor space, stacking the bottles high within its narrow confines. Display arches and rounded corners make sure that the space still packs lots of impressive visual impact. *Courtesy of Grotto Custom Wine Cellars & Cabinets*

T he average age of a French oak tree harvested for use in wine barrel construction is 170 years. Only five percent of the tree is suitable for making these barrels.

A wonderful effect is achieved by setting racking flush with the wall. *Courtesy of Wine Cellar Innovations*

An inspiring view is framed by the attractive curves of wine bottles. *Courtesy of Apex Wine Cellars & Racking Systems*

A five-sided alcove houses an impressive collection. *Courtesy of Wine Cellar Innovations*

A semi-circular alcove seals off behind French doors. *Courtesy of Vinotemp International Corp.*

Just off a dining area, a wine cellar
beckons with its impressive collection.
Courtesy of Artistic Wine Cellar

A wine cellar is essentially a hobby room, outfitted to satisfy the urges of a connoisseur to spend time cataloging and caring for a collection in anticipation of the moment when a treasure will be uncorked. *Courtesy of Sleeping Grape Wine Cellars*

Courtesy of Fine Woodworking

176

R ed wines need to breathe a bit before being served, though less time is needed for older wines. Fill a wine glass to its widest part. Avoid filling too far as this will limit the "swirl." Swirl the wine around in your glass before tasting it to reveal its aroma. The fragrance is part of the enjoyment one gets from drinking wine.

Small, electric units create different temperature controls within this wine closet. *Courtesy of Sleeping Grape Wine Cellars*

A wine cellar is handy to the kitchen, located beyond a barrier of glass and stone wall. *Courtesy of Valentini's Custom Wine Cellars*

A cellar area is visually accessible without breaching the temperature and humidity barrier. Because the bottles are so close at hand, and stored with their labels facing out on open wire racks, the owner can minimize his intrusion into their space. *Courtesy of Grotto Custom Wine Cellars & Cabinets*

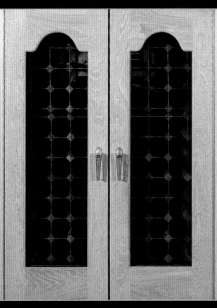

A multitude of wine storage units are being designed for display in any room of the home, in styles to match fine furnishings. Credenza-sized units are a nice addition along a dining room wall, or almost any room of the home. *Courtesy of Vinotemp International Corp.*

A custome wine cabinet is the perfet fit for a Tuscan-style kitchen.
Courtesy of Wood Mode Cabinetry

181

A wine cellar repre-
sents an accumu-
lated knowledge
of wine, washed in nostal-
gic memories shared with
friends and family. Wine is
perhaps the most social of
investment endeavors. In
this case, the investor packs
away something wonderful,
expecting it to grow more
so in anticipation of a time
when he can share it with
others.

An undercounter, stainless steel wine cabinet is perfectly
at home within the settings of two very different kitchens.
Courtesy of Viking Range Corporation

Under-counter wine storage is a big trend in the modern kitchen. *Courtesy of Viking Range Corporation*

A small wine refrigerator allow you to store up to 28 bottles on the countertop. *Courtesy of Vinotemp International Corp.*

184

Courtesy of Wood Mode Custom Cabinetry

Wine, ready to consume, is stored in decorative diamond racks in the kitchen. *Courtesy of Wood Mode Custom Cabinetry*

Wall units are a wonderful option for starter collections, or for keeping soon-to-consume bottles close at hand. *Courtesy of Viking Range Corporation*

A wine storage unti tucks neatly into the end of a central island workstation.
Courtesy of Wood Mode Custom Cabinetry

187

Red wines work wonderfully with rich food and dark meats. White complements chicken and seafood. If you are choosing a wine to go with a variety of foods, try a subtle Pinot Noir or Chardonnay.

Duel displays of half-round shelves form a focal point in this cellar. *Courtesy of Wine Cellar Innovations*

Rich tones and a shaded chandelier add to the stately sense of establishment in this cellar. The addition of a wet bar makes clean-up after uncorking and tasting a far simpler task. *Courtesy of Wine Cellar Innovations*

I t isn't advisable to spend a lot of time in your cellar – after all, your entry and your presence have an effect on the room's temperature and humidity. But it doesn't hurt to visit sometimes, or to bring a friend along. Here are cellars set up to host friends for intimate tastings, and maybe a little food and music to liven the mix.

Dual undercounter coolers, and diamond racking sport a collection of vintages kept at the ready in a tasting area of the home. *Courtesy of Wood Mode Custom Cabinetry*

Wine is revered, if not perfectly preserved, in a hobby room
where music and literature also enjoy a prominent role.
Courtesy of Beasley & Henley Interior Design

He who loves not wine, women, and song remains a fool his whole life long.

~Martin Luther

Make your guests feel as if they've entered a castle with a stone ceiling and old-fashioned wooden chairs and table. *Courtesy of Apex Wine Cellars & Racking Systems*

Steel grape vines adorn the glass portal to this lovely wine cellar.
Courtesy of Apex Wine Cellars & Racking Systems

Decanting wine softens a younger vintage, and allows an older wine to separate from the built-up sediment. Allow a young red to breathe, pouring it into a glass, giving it a swirl, and allowing it to rest for a few minutes before drinking.

Racking negotiates a corner with a curve, mirrored in the paneled ceiling above. *Courtesy of Wine Cellar Innovations*

Take a trip back in time with a display that mimics wine vaults of centuries ago. A bar accommodates half a dozen tasters beneath an impressive stone ceiling. *Courtesy of Dalst Stone Wine Cellars*

Today's top restaurants know the value of having a wine steward on staff and an impressive collection on hand for educated patrons. Images of restaurants, as well as racking systems found in hotels and commercial wineries, are inspiring for those hoping to someday house a comparable collection.

Restaurant patrons are allowed visual access to the wine collection.
Courtesy of Hirschberg Design Group

A huge collection makes selection of the
evening's vintage an adventure.
Courtesy of Rosehill Wine Cellars

If all be true that I do think,
      There are five reasons we should drink:
    Good wine, a friend, or being dry
    Or lest we should be by and by
    Or any other reason why.

~Henry Aldrich

Courtesy of Rosehill Wine Cellars

A visual knockout, this wine vault revolves around a central
display unit capped by a counter with a gorgeous marble
inset. *Courtesy of Doc Watters Wine Cellars, Inc.*

People and delicate, aging wines shouldn't mix. For this reason, patrons of the Wine Cellar in this upscale hotel are separated by glass during special tastings. *Courtesy of Paul Wyatt Designs*

207

A̶ge appears to be best in four things: old wood best to burn, old wine to drink, old friends to trust, and old authors to read."

~Alonson of Aragon

Courtesy of Paul Wyatt Designs

A cave-like limestone vault houses bottles in stock by a French vintner.
Courtesy of Dalst Stone Wine Cellars

Sauvignon blanc and Riesling tend to lose their aroma in a big red wine glass, but heavily oaked red wines need bigger glasses to show off their more robust flavors.

Imported limestone racking furnishes a showroom. *Courtesy of Dalst Stone Wine Cellars*

The passageways to a wine storage area are
appropriately medieval, setting the tone for
the treasures stored beyond. Hand-hewn beams
support the ceiling, and the cellar is lit by
sconces crafted from hand-forged iron.
Courtesy of Germano Custom Wine Cellars

All of the accouterments
are appropriately ancient
in feel, adding to the
enjoyment of vintages
aging on open racks. The
coin corners or toothing
are made of Ohio state
limestone, which are
bush hammered. The
arches, walk through,
and columns are native
fieldstone from the
owner's property. Rubble
stone fill was used
between the stones.
Courtesy of Germano
Custom Wine Cellars

Wine will look its age. White wines progress from a light straw color to a deep golden color as they get older. Reds start out as deep purple colors and progress to brown and rust colors as they age. Clarity indicates quality.

Courtesy of Apex Wine Cellars & Racking Systems

216

Ceramic terracotta racks can be stacked and mortared for a classic wine cellar feel. *Courtesy of Vinotemp International Corp*

A wonderful, carved table and comfy chairs make this a welcoming center, perfect for sharing an uncorking with a dear friend. *Courtesy of Wine Cellar Innovations*

Resource Guide

Alan's Wine Cellar
50 Altamont Avenue
Mill Valley, CA 94941
415-381-1784
www.alanswinecellar.com

Apex Wine Cellars & Racking Systems
15540 Woodinville-Redmont Rd., A-800
Woodinville, WA 98072
425-398-0565 / 888-999-9749
www.apexwinecellars.com

Artistic Wine Cellars
4286 Redwood Highway
San Rafael, CA 94903
415-492-1450
www.artisticcellars.com

Atwood: Fine Architectural Cabinetry
633 South Main Street
Greenville, SC 29601
864-233-3730
www.atwoodcabinetry.com

Beasley & Henley Interior Design
IB1038
919 Orange Ave.
Winter Park, FL 32789
407-629-7756
www.beasleyandhenley.com

Burrowing Owl Winery
100 Burrowing Owl Place
RR#1 Site 52 Comp 20
Oliver, BC, V0H-ITO
877-498-0620
info@burrowingowlonline.ca

Dalst Stone Wine Cellars
P.O. Box 465
Roxbury, NY 12474
607-326-3040
www.dalst.com

Doc Watters Wine Cellars, Inc.
1145 W. Custer Place Unit B
Denver, CO 80223
720-435-5102
office: 303-435-5102

Eldorado Stone
1370 Grand Ave. #B
San Marcos, CA 92078
800-925-1491 for customers
760-213-5686
www.eldoradostone.com

Germano Custom Wine Cellars
1331 Carter's Creek Pike
Columbia, TN 38401
615-586-2142
www.germanowinecellars.com

Grotto Custom Wine Cellars & Cabinets
27121 Aliso Creek Road, Suite 125
Aliso Viejo, CA 92656
866-Cool-Wine
www.GrottoCellars.com

Hirschberg Design Group, Inc.
334 Queen Street E.
Toronto, Ontario M5A 1S8 Canada
(p) 416-868-1210
www.hirschbergdesign.com

Northbay Kitchen
822 Peteluma Blvd. N.
Peteluma, CA 94952
707-769-1646

Paul Wyatt Designs, LLC
Fine Wine Rack and Cellar Company
295 S. 250 E.
Burley, ID 83318
888-654-4055
www.fine-wine.com
www.paulwyatt.com

Rosehill Wine Cellars, Inc.
339 Olivewood Road
Toronto, Ontario M8Z 2Z6 Canada
888-253-6807/416-285-6604
www.rosehillwinecellars.com

Sleeping Grape Wine Cellars
#10-650 Roche Point Road
North Vancouver B.C., V7H 2Z5
604-790-8893
www.sleepinggrape.com

Steven Paul Whitsitt Photography
6 Ainsworth Court
Durham, NC 27713
919-572-0650
whitsittphoto@yahoo.com

Valentini Custom Wine Cellars
128 Bison Avenue, B940
Newport Beach, CA 92660
888.330.6371 phone
Kat4wine@aol.com

Vicarage Wine Cellars
The Old Vicarage
Ridgeway Moor, Ridgeway Village
Sheffield S12 3XW UK
0114-2475814
wines@theoldvicarage.co.uk

Viking Range Corporation
111 Front Street
Greenwood, Mississippi 38930 USA
1-888-845-4641
www.vikingrange.com

Vinotemp International Corp.
17631 South Susana Road
Rancho Dominguez, CA 90221
800-777-8466

Vinotéque
1738 E. Alpine Avenue
Stockton, CA 95205
800-343-9463
www.vinotheque.com

Wellborn Forest Fine Kitchen
Cabinetry
2212 Airport Boulevard
Alexander City, AL 35010
800-846-2562
www.wellbornforest.com
Designer: Rick Grinder; www.
designerrick.com

Wine Cellar Innovations
4575 Eastern Ave.
Cincinnati, OH 45226
800-229-9813
winecellarinnovations.com
WineRacks.com Inc.
P.O. Box 67
High Falls, NY 12440
1-888-687-2517

Wood Mode Custom Cabinetry
One Second Street
Kreamer, PA 17833
800-635-7500
www.wood-mode.com